G000240978

The Ghosts of
EXETER

Sally & Chips Barber

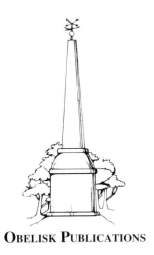

OBELISK PUBLICATIONS

ALSO BY THE AUTHORS

The Lost City of Exeter / The Great Little Exeter Book
Beautiful Exeter / Topsham Past and Present
Around & About the Haldon Hills–Revisited
Diary of a Dartmoor Walker / Diary of a Devonshire Walker
The Great Little Dartmoor Book / The Great Little Totnes Book
Made in Devon / Burgh Island and Bigbury Bay
Dark & Dastardly Dartmoor / Weird and Wonderful Dartmoor
Tales of the Teign / The Great Little Chagford Book
Ten Family Walks on Dartmoor / Ten Family Walks in East Devon
Six Short Pub Walks on Dartmoor
The Great Little Plymouth Book / Plymouth in Colour
Ghastly and Ghostly Devon / Dawlish and Dawlish Warren
The South Hams / Beautiful Dartmoor
Torquay / Paignton / Brixham
Around & About Salcombe / Around & About Seaton and Beer
Around & About Sidmouth / Around & About Teignmouth and Shaldon
From the Dart to the Start / Dartmouth and Kingswear
Cranmere Pool – the First Dartmoor Letterbox
Haunted Pubs in Devon
Brixham of Yesteryear Parts I, II and III
Teign Valley of Yesteryear Parts I and II
Princetown of Yesteryear Parts I and II
Pinhoe of Yesteryear Parts I and II
Torbay in Colour – Torquay, Paignton, Brixham
Widecombe – A Visitor's Guide
Newton Ferrers & Noss Mayo
Along The Otter

We have over 140 Devon titles; for further details please send SAE to
Obelisk Publications, 2 Church Hill, Pinhoe, Exeter, EX4 9ER,
or telephone (01392) 468556

Acknowledgments

Thanks to everybody who furnished us with stories, both in the previous edition and this new revised version. Thanks also to Jane Reynolds for cover illustrations and drawings on pages 21, 25, 27, 28, 29 and 32. All photographs are by or belong to Chips Barber apart from page 31 supplied by Devon Library Services.

First published in 1990
ISBN: 0 946651 35 3
This revised edition published in 1996 by
Obelisk Publications, 2 Church Hill, Pinhoe, Exeter, Devon
Designed and Typeset by Sally Barber
Printed in Great Britain by
The Devonshire Press Limited, Torquay, Devon

© Sally & Chips Barber 1996

Introduction

Statistically more ghosts and apparitions are seen by people in Britain than in any other country. Apparently one in every ten people will either see a ghost or experience a spectral or supernatural occurrence sometime in their lifetime. This suggests that almost ten thousand Exonians will one day, or probably night, see or feel a ghost! Obviously then this collection is just the tip of the proverbial iceberg when it comes to the storytelling of Exeter's ghosts.

Since *The Ghosts of Exeter* was first published, specialised ghost tours have been established in the city centre, conducted by the 'Redcoat' guides who are all fully trained volunteers. Without doubt they have proved to be immensely popular even though they do not employ the same theatrical touch as those who organise ghost tours in the haunted city of York. There 'actors', dressed as ghosts, pounce out of dark alleyways, scaring those who come to hear about them. However, whilst such scary, spirit safaris are good fun, we feel the more sedate, sophisticated spiritual soirées of Exeter have a more genuine feel about them.

The Ghostliest City?

Although York claims to contain Britain's most haunted square mile, Exeter must surely run close to it for in and around the Cathedral precincts alone there is a surplus of spooks. The author Bram Stoker, who wrote *Dracula*, chose Exeter's Cathedral Close as the place from where the young solicitor, Jonathan Harker, leaves to go to Transylvania – fortunately Dracula is not enticed back to Exeter in the story! However, perhaps we should concentrate ourselves on getting *our* teeth into some of the many real scary stories that abound in this hallowed corner of Exeter.

Broadgate's Friendly Fred!

Long ago this part of Exeter was inaccessible at night for the seven gates which protected the Cathedral area were all closed tight to keep out intruders – a wall within a walled city. The most important gate was Broadgate, the location of which is now marked by a stone just off the High Street. It is opposite 'Tinleys', once a household name (now Pizza Express), a building that is much older than its façade suggests. The story goes that the gatekeeper at Broadgate neglected his duty one night and an assassin stole into the Cathedral to commit a dark and dastardly deed, and crept away again undetected. In the morning the gate was still ajar, the sleeping gatekeeper was arrested and, along with the Mayor, found guilty of neglect and executed. It is believed to be the gatekeeper, now fondly known as 'Fred', who stalks the Tinleys building but, apart from rumblings, footsteps and unaccountable knockings, he does not seem to cause anyone any harm. One flaw in the story is that it was the South Gate that was left open!

Ship Inn – Naughty Sir Francis!

Martin's Lane is the narrow thoroughfare that links the High Street to the Cathedral

area. The Ship Inn is a timbered inn along it, which has always boasted its connection with one of England's most famous Elizabethans. It is believed that the likes of England's greatest Elizabethan sea dogs met either in the building nearby, known as Mol's Coffee House (now housing Nottingham and Walsh) or in the Ship Inn and, according to various accounts, still do. Many Elizabethan ghosts have been sighted in this vicinity, not least Drake himself, a man who did nothing by halves (just pints). Rumour hath it that as the great man quaffed far too much ale for his own good, he was only permitted to drink there if accompanied by a responsible person. Perhaps this affront to so great a personage is the reason for him causing mayhem and mischief at the historic Ship Inn, for it is suggested that he has nudged people down flights of stairs and has been a mischievous nuisance in an inn that he himself described as his favourite place, next to his 'own shippe'.

Cathedral Close – Very Close!

There never was anyone more level-headed than the late Right Reverend Wilfred Westall, a former Bishop of Crediton. This most eminent and likable man resided at

Number 10, Cathedral Close, the official residence of the Bishop of Crediton, and he maintained that the property was definitely haunted, particularly one bedroom. The bedroom door was a heavy one and was often prone to open, despite a lack of draught, and would also close itself when left open. On other occasions heavy breathing could be clearly heard, a fact borne out over a period of years by a variety of witnesses.

The Front Cover Picture Story!

The next tale has all the ingredients of a "True Romance" story. The two main characters of the plot are a pious monk called John, whose probable job involved the embalming of the dead and who took his vows with a good strong faith, and a nun called Martha whose work brought her to the Cathedral area. Needless to say a glance here and a glance there resulted in the two falling 'head over heels' in love. Alas these entirely natural feelings were totally against their chosen vocations. Realising the potency of their emotions, poor John the Monk and Martha the Nun decided the only way out of their wretched predicament was to jump down a well at John's abode, Number 5, Cathedral Close. A pact was made and the two frustrated lovers drowned themselves; although they could not be together in this life, they could at least become united in eternity.

This is a touching story of far-reaching devotion but it may have been the easier option for it is believed that those who had taken holy vows could be sentenced to being walled up alive if it were discovered that they harboured amorous feelings!

For years these premises housed the former Exeter and County Club. Various workers had strange experiences here but one employee in particular, a sensible young lady, who readily admitted to having been sceptical of the existence of ghosts, is now definitely in no doubt as to their actuality. Her change of opinion stemmed back to one occasion when she had reason to go down to the cellar. Here she suddenly smelt a strange aroma in the air, which she later realised was rose water. On returning upstairs she asked another worker to go down to see if she could notice anything. Several moments later the colleague returned with her face ashen white – as if she had seen a ghost. She too had sniffed the rose water scent but, more disturbingly, she had also felt a strange presence, which had literally stood face to face with her. Needless to say, both girls were obviously scared by the experience yet, as the months passed by uneventfully they forgot their ordeal.

However, early one evening the same girl was working in the bar when she felt a draught on her face, and instantly looked around for an open door or window – there was none. Seconds later she felt the same sensation that you get when someone blows into your face from an adjacent spot. Her immediate reaction was to take a step back but she found she couldn't put her heel down to the ground. In a panic she ran from the bar in order to phone her husband for help. She tried the number and the line was dead, so then she dialled her mother, then her sister – each time with the same result, or lack of it. Inadvertently she gazed down at the floor and she saw a long and pointed cloth shoe. Not wishing to witness any more of this grim spectre, she hurried from the building, turning off and closing what she could on the way, to reach the sanctuary of the outside world. Today she works elsewhere!

Many years ago 'Diana' was a frequent visitor to another house in the Cathedral Close. The visits were usually enjoyable experiences but for one detail. There was a room at the top of two flights of stairs, overlooking the Cathedral Green, which was always unnaturally cold. It was so spooky and icy in fact that it was decided to lock the room and leave it unused so that any malevolent forces could be left to brood alone.

A Modest Ghost

Just across the Green at Number 18 Cathedral Yard is Michelmore's, Solicitors and Notaries Public, an old and long-established firm. The building has a serious air but its resident ghost has a comic-like appearance and has been seen on a few occasions in recent years. One of the more recent sightings was by an employee of Jaegers, who also used the same building, and a cleaner, who witnessed the spectacle together.

Picture if you can the ghost of a man, about 60 years old, sporting an old-fashioned nightcap à la Wee Willie Winkie. To complete his garb, a long night shirt went down to his kneecaps but was of such a generous capacity that a little waft of air in an upward direction might have caused this pale spectre to blush with embarrassment. And lo, this apparition showed itself to these ladies, hurriedly materialising out of one door to disappear into the Gent's toilet in a desperate fashion. In his great haste his posture was somewhat bent over to hold the lower part of his nightie shut at the knees – in order to preserve his modesty. Strangely, although this ghost had legs, he had no feet! The two witnesses were startled, one fled in fear whilst the other was too agog to do anything although, needless to say, she didn't inspect the toilet to see if the apparition had finished his business! One wonders under what circumstances this poor chap could have been caught out, unless it was at a time when he had imbibed too many spirits for his own good!

The Globe Hotel – Rather Swish

The Globe Hotel has gone and, we believe, so has its ghostly problem. It stood in the south west corner of the Cathedral Yard and was regarded as one of the foremost hotels in the City. Its hauntings were largely in the 1930s when guests were awoken from their slumbers by swishing and swirling noises that could not be explained. The late seventeenth-century building, which boasted a Tudor period oak-panelled smoke lounge and electric light, was gutted by fire during the Second World War. Attempts to save it proved futile and its shell was pulled down. Today it is possible to walk right through the place where it stood as it is now a thoroughfare from the Cathedral Yard through to the top of South Street. Keep your ears open for the sound of the swishing and swirling – it will most likely be one of Exeter's many minibuses whizzing past!

A Cathedral Couple

The Cathedral has seen its share of hauntings, which is hardly surprising as it has had such a long history. Those who work in and around the Cathedral often do so because of their love for this wonderful edifice. A past verger, who had acquired a great knowledge and affection for the place, has been seen a few times since his untimely death. He has appeared in one of the chapels although, surprisingly, it is not known to have been one of his favourites. Two independent persons, one now passed on, the other still involved in the day-to-day work of the Cathedral, both told of how they had seen this ghost. These sightings had been in the same chapel, the stories matching in every detail. Neither person had known about the other's experience!

Another haunting, seen in the heat of a July evening throughout many years, has been the ghost of a nun, seen flowing in a floating fashion from the south wall of the nave, only to merge into a wall of the Church House. No theories have been offered up as to the reason for her hauntings.

Other Cathedral Ghosts

In the autumn of 1995, before the 6.30 p.m. service, all was quiet in the Cathedral until the ghost of a gentleman, wearing a plum-coloured cassock, was spotted heading from

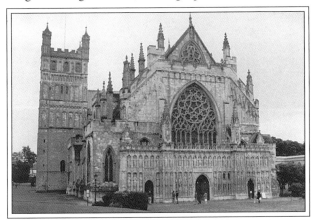

the Lady Chapel towards the vestry, which it entered. The witness was somewhat taken aback at what he had seen but had the presence of mind to hurry along to see who the short person may have been. Although there was no other unlocked exit from this room, an inspection revealed that there was nobody there!

Several people who, through their work, spend long periods of time in the Cathedral, have heard a chatty ghost with a limited vocabulary for its party piece is to say a friendly 'Hello'. This disembodied sound has often been heard in the vicinity of St James Chapel and the verger's office.

Another, equally inexplicable, occurrence was also noted by more than one person when a strange apparition, which can only be described as a black shape, was seen passing in front of the nave altar. It was shaped like a human and moved at speed, nobody being able to determine who or what it was.

During a service at Easter, one of those present felt his arm tugged and, believing he knew who it was, turned around to find nobody there … the person it should have been was on the far side of the Cathedral! After the service he related the experience to some others. To his surprise a lady verger confirmed that when she had been in that same spot she, too, had also had her sleeve tugged.

The Cathedral is an immense structure with various chapels. At St Catherine's it has been rumoured that the ghosts of two lovers have been seen, whilst in St Gabriel's some who have ventured in have felt compelled to leave, almost as if they were being pushed out!

Shoe Shop with a Soul or Two

The High Street has also got its fair share of ghosts and the section from the junction at the top of Fore/South and North Streets as far as St Stephen's Church is an extremely old one. If its buildings could talk, and it's just as well that they don't, they could tell some amazing tales! Just to the south of the Guildhall, on the same side of the street, is Oliver's Shoe Shop, which is very well managed by Paul Holland. He believes that the cellar is haunted by the ghost of a dog. Perhaps it is the original hush puppy?

A Boozy old Ghost

The Turk's Head, next door to the shoe shop, is famous for its connections with Charles Dickens who spent quite a bit of time here, all the while mindful of collecting

new characters to fill his many literary works. There are some who say that he haunts the building but there are no positive sightings that we can quote chapter and verse. However, this ancient building, beside Exeter's Guildhall, does have one ghost who sees the obvious advantages of 'living' in a pub.

The ghost, that made many appearances in the early 1980s, was a red-haired lady wearing a most beautiful gown. According to Mrs Andrews, a former barmaid of the Turk's Head, the poor lady never looked very happy, the thought being that she committed suicide here. The ghost has been accused of trying to drown her sorrows for the optic doling out gin had emptied itself on a number of occasions, the red-haired lady being deemed responsible for this.

Mrs Andrews later worked at the Devon and Exeter Institution in the Cathedral Close. Both she and her husband saw one of the ghosts to haunt this building. Sometimes in the morning a ghostly sailor would be spied, sitting down reading a newspaper. He was described as being in the uniform of Nelson's day.

Exeter's Clumsiest Ghost

The Guildhall, next door to the Turk's Head, is the focal point of attention for visitors strolling up the High Street. Its distinct frontage makes it a favourite with tourists who have an eye for a historic souvenir snap of their visit to the city. Immediately beside it, on the right as you face the Guildhall, is a modern jeweller's shop, previously called Zales but now Ernest Jones. It was once connected to the Guildhall by virtue of its basement having been part of the original dungeon prison that ran from The Turk's Head, below street level, to the shop. It was here, below ground level, and in the days when it was a clothes shop, where strange, unaccountable things happened. The manager and his assistant were startled by a spectral head which came, at speed, towards them, vanishing into thin air just a few feet from them. On another occasion a shop assistant heard racks of clothes being shunted around but knew nobody should have been down in the stock room. On investigation

she was confronted by the complete ghost of a lady dressed in costume from a time well over two centuries ago. She too disappeared suddenly.

In the late 1980s the employees of Zales, who took over the premises, also experienced visitations. The nature of the hauntings changed but it is believed that, generally, the resident ghost is a friendly female. However, she takes an obvious delight in being mischievous (or clumsy) as she been known to trigger the fire alarm on numerous occasions, and kept knocking items over, making loud bumps in the cellar, usually when there was nobody around. One fainthearted male employee refused to go down there after sensing a presence and two decorators, who had previously done work in the basement when it was a clothes shop, also inquired first whether the ghost was still down there!

The Ghost of a Real Queen

Exeter suffered a lot of damage during the blitz, large parts of the city centre being razed to the ground. Many fine buildings were either lost or so badly damaged that they were later demolished.

Bampfylde House was a fine home at one time, belonging to Lord Poltimore who owned many properties in Devon. The house has gone but when it stood just off Bedford Street it had its spooky moments.

In the period between the two World Wars it was a sort of small museum with various items of interest for members of the public to inspect, one of these being a very old, tall-backed chair. The curator invited a lady to sit on it. He was surprised that the posture she adopted was the correct one for such a seat. However, as he watched her a change came over her face as she peered out of the window with great concentration. Her face turned ashen white and her eyes filled with tears, the lady finding it hard to stem the flow. As she gazed out she said, "Oh, the poor thing!" But the curator was stumped because he could clearly see that there was nobody there. There wasn't much he could say for he could see the lady was genuine with her emotions. After a while the colour returned to her cheeks and he felt that it would be reasonable to ask her about what had happened. She explained to him that she saw a fragile-looking lady wearing the costume of the day from the seventeenth century.

It may sound like a romantic notion for the ghost of Queen Henrietta Maria, wife of Charles I, to haunt a part of Exeter but in the first half of the seventeenth century, the heavily pregnant Queen took sanctuary in Exeter. This was in 1644 during the English Civil War and Exeter was an excellent choice of location for what was to be the royal pair's sixth child. The Queen took up residence in Bedford House, close to the site of Exeter's main post office today. On 16 June she gave birth to a daughter, Princess Henrietta Anne. She was baptised in a specially erected font in Exeter Cathedral on 21 July. Her mother missed the occasion because the Earl of Essex and his Parliamentarian troops were approaching Exeter so she fled to Falmouth and sailed to France. It could just be possible that the trauma of this episode in her life was enough to call her back to Exeter in a ghostly form. According to documentation in 1962, it is be-

Princess Henrietta Anne as depicted on the High Street

lieved that the Queen was positively identified walking through the gardens of Barnfield

House. She was spotted as a fragile looking woman who simply vanished into thin air before the eyes of the witness. So it is equally possible that her ghost was seen from the window of Bampfylde House, looking towards Bedford House where she stayed.

Hello Sailor!

Sometimes a 'ghost' can be so real that, if it happens to be someone you know, you are not prepared to accept it could be a ghost until you have proof that it could have been nothing else! This is what happened to a local man during the last war.

Vincent Wills worked in a small bakery in Paris Street and became very friendly with a young lad who was awaiting call-up in the Royal Navy so helped them out temporarily over a busy holiday period. He left them after nine weeks, underwent six weeks' shore training, and then was posted to convoy duty in the English Channel. Sadly, after just a few weeks, his ship was torpedoed and he was reported missing, presumed dead. Then, one gloomy winter evening, Vincent and his retired father were snoozing by the fire when the young sailor walked into the room. Naturally Vincent was delighted but when he jumped up to greet him, the lad walked straight past him, through the house, out the back and into Vincent's cousin's house, the manager of the bakery. Rushing after him to hear his news, Vincent was astounded to discover that his cousin and family had seen no one enter their house and said Vincent had obviously been dreaming. Thoroughly bemused, and wondering if he had perhaps conjured him up in his own mind, he returned home – and his father asked him who the young sailor was that had walked through the room!

A full account, in Vincent Wills' own words, is given in *Haunted Happenings in Devon*, and is well worth reading!

Grave Situation?

It is surprising to note that graveyards and hospitals do not appear to throw up as many ghosts as one might expect. The former could be explained because most of the witnesses to any hauntings would themselves be dead, and of course dead men tell no tales. Also perhaps, people sensitive to such happenings would consciously avoid graveyards. But hospitals are places where, all too often, people are exposed to traumatic sufferings, commonly thought to be the basis of 'unquiet spirits'.

As far as Exeter is concerned only a few tales have emerged. At the old Royal Devon and Exeter Hospital in Southernhay, now Dean Clark House, are the well-known ghosts of the Grey Lady, who has made many appearances, and also the spectre of 'The Matron' who has loomed large at times. Apart from being seen by numerous people, the Grey Lady has also been 'seen' in her invisible form when she rushes down ward corridors flinging open heavy doors with apparent effortlessness. People with psychic powers have been known to talk with her, only to have been labelled as 'cranks' for talking to an invisible host.

Illya Nastase, not to be confused with Ilie Nastase the one-time tennis ace, worked there when it was a hospital. He recalled cleaning the main theatre late one night when he just knew he was being watched and lifted his eyes up to catch the sight of a woman's head peering through one of the glass panels of the door. Suspecting that she shouldn't have been there, he put down his bucket and moved swiftly to the door. In the corridor, of an almost empty late night hospital, he looked in disbelief as there was nobody there. He believed that his encounter had been with the Matron, perhaps checking to see that the theatre was being cleaned in readiness for the next day's operations.

On another occasion he was working in an area of the hospital not far from the intensive care ward. He looked up to see a grey person rushing past him looking in a most perplexed state as she disappeared in that direction. An immediate enquiry led to the discovery that nobody had entered that ward.

Although Illya is the first to admit that he really shouldn't have used the recovery room for an occasional few winks of sleep, he did so a few times when the opportunity and the need coincided. One such time he was rudely awoken from his slumbers by the sounds of rattling trolleys. When he came to his senses he realised that the disturbance wasn't caused by human interference but by some invisible force that gave him quite a fright. He didn't repeat the deed again!

At Heavitree's hospital it is believed that the ghost of a young girl, who died after a long stay, visits an old people's ward. She has been known to sit on the beds of various patients and comfort them. At other times she has been seen by nurses playing with a ball in corridors.

House of Sighs

North Street, earlier this century, was a rough and tumble thoroughfare with plenty of small shops and family businesses. All around were people living in tenements, cluttered courtyards or working-class dwellings. However, the people that lived there were forthright and honest and therefore not given to exaggeration.

Opposite what was a public house, called The Elephant, was a small fruit and vegetable shop whose occupants lived above the premises. In keeping with the way families tended to root and stay in one place, this family had been there for many years when, in the 1960s, a series of unusual and inexplicable events occurred in the upper part of the building.

There were two staircases, one at the front and another at the back, which was for the servants' use in Victorian times, when the buildings in the street were town houses for merchants and wealthy traders. On climbing the main stairs one evening the lady of the house opened the door of her bedroom, situated at the front of the house. As she did so a spectral, highly-illuminated shape swiftly passed across the room, almost in a flash. This happened again on other occasions and, despite research into the matter, no conclusions could be drawn as to the origin or cause of such a strange, bright phenomenon occurring inside a bedroom with the curtains fully drawn.

Some time later the same lady and her daughter were respectively at the front and back extremes of the property, on the sort of day you could hear a pin drop. Somewhere between the two a very obvious and elongated sigh could be clearly heard by both ladies. Each thought it was the other and went onto the landing to find out why. But on quizzing each other they were both aghast to find it was neither of them. The memory of this has lingered, very clearly, with them ever since.

Mrs White's Grey Ghost

In the area in and around Exeter's Iron Bridge are some old properties. These are the ones that have survived the drastic redevelopment that has taken place in the Exe Street and Mount Dinham vicinity. Although you might think that the ghostliest place in Exeter

would be the spooky looking catacombs, they are in fact not haunted whilst a meek and mild little house not far from them is.

The Whites first saw the house when it was up for sale and although it didn't look old from the outside, it did in fact possess many 'character' facets inside. Experts dated it at mid-seventeenth century. After inspecting the property they agreed to buy and some months later moved in. One of the members of the family had not been entirely happy about the feel of the house but convinced herself that she was probably being silly so put the thought firmly at the back of her mind.

Haunted Pub?

All went well and the house gradually was rearranged to suit the Whites. A builder was brought in for some major structural work and at the end of his three-month stint confessed to the family that whenever he was in a certain part of the house he felt most uncomfortable. Mrs

White too shared this feeling of a chilly presence each time she crossed the landing late at night and her fears were eventually confirmed when her son came home from University for a vacation. He was given a bedroom on an upper level and one night he was rudely awoken by a youngish woman in a long grey skirt who scowled at him in a disapproving fashion as though he had no right to be there. The poor lad was greatly distressed by this experience and refused to sleep in the dark in the house again and always had to have a light left on. His mother never got to see the ghost but distinctly felt the ghost's long skirt brush against her bare legs on two occasions, late at night, on the landing. Fortunately nothing has ever happened with lights on, or in any other part of the house.

Superghost!

The stream that runs through the green fields of the Hoopern valley, below the University of Exeter's main campus, is called the Taddiforde Brook, 'taddy' being possibly a corruption of 'toad'. Off New North Road, which runs over this stream, there are various addresses that are preceded by Taddiforde, some accessible only through a somewhat sinister-looking arch.

A large house, also of the same name, was built late in the nineteenth century, to be the incredible home of Mr Kent Kingdon, an eccentric religious man who occasionally dabbled in magic. He was a skilled craftsman and used his skills to good effect inside his mansion. In particular one staircase that rose inside a tower was beautifully crafted. Doors leading off of it were inscribed with various biblical edicts of how one should live. Some people believe that when Kent Kingdon died he was buried in the grounds but later his bones were dug up and re-interred in the nearby St David's churchyard. Other sources claim that he was buried either in or near the arch at the entrance of his small estate. People unaware of this story have often felt a shiver passing down their spine when passing by the arch.

Mr Kingdon's ghost has been back to the house. He appeared to a young child once, standing by her bed and gazing down at her for a few seconds before fading away.

The lady who bought the house, on his demise, was just as eccentric but it is not known whether she makes ghostly appearances. Miss Morrison showed her eccentricity by employing a chauffeur but rarely allowing him to drive her Mercedes Benz, this she did herself, leaving him the pleasure of washing it! She really was quite a driver because in 1914 she won the Paris Grand Prix! She was less religious than her predecessor at the mansion and 'converted' his chapel into a casino. So it would be no surprise for his restless soul to haunt the place!

The Brewery Beast

For twenty-three long years the basement of the St Anne's Well Brewery, which lies beneath the North or Iron Bridge, had remained undisturbed, the brewers having been put out of business by market rather than unnatural forces. Beneath such headlines as "Labourers Too Scared to Work" and "Something Stirs Deep in the Cellar" a story unfolded concerning some strange events, enough to cause one worker to walk out on the job of converting the space into a restaurant, never to return. Several tough building labourers were scared out of their wits by seeing such spectacles as large iron bars of great weight and potential danger, hurling themselves around, hosepipes suddenly whiplashing into the air and, even more disconcerting, large unaccountable footprints suddenly appearing in sand lying on the floor. A revolt amongst the workers caused a slight labour problem for the landlord as six of the men refused to work night shifts, a time when terrifying cries were also heard here, said to sound like someone falling to

their death. The remaining lads showed true British stoicism, however, by saying that they all felt a lot better after they'd had a cup of tea to calm them down! The pub in this building is now 'The Fizgig and Firkin'.

Another pub with a ghost is the Papermakers, just a little way down the valley, at the other end of Exe Street. Its name comes from the former paper-making factory, which stood opposite on the river side of adjacent Bonhay Road. The pub, which has always been called the Papermakers, has existed since 1820 and its clientèle will have changed since the factory closed in 1967. The ghost is not that of a former paper-maker but a previous landlord. The current owner, Mr Ellis, could hardly believe his eyes when the ghost strolled slowly along an upstairs corridor. The ghostly image was a man of about forty, from the Edwardian era. He had bushy hair and spectacles and made no effort to hurry as he casually walked straight through the wall, much to Mr Ellis's amazement. Naturally the owner has endeavoured to discover who this may have been. It has been suggested that this was a landlord who committed suicide here but to date this has not been verified. There are many pubs which are haunted – hardly surprising to note when 'they are licensed for spirits!' If you want to discover more then our book *Haunted Pubs in Devon* will throw the doors open to many others.

The Ghosts of Exeter

Best Cellar?

The otherwise sober area around Bartholomew Street, just inside the city wall, and high on the slope above Exe Street, is one of the oldest inhabited parts of the city and is where the first settlement in the area was born  before the Romans arrived. However, that is just an irrelevant snippet of information for the ghosts of 2 Bartholomew Terrace were at their most active in 1939. At that time a prison officer lived there with his family, which consisted of his wife, a son, a daughter and the dog. The father and daughter were not unduly troubled by the presence in the house but the son and the mother were sensitive and knew that things were not as they should be. The problems occurred whenever the dog was let out into the back garden for 'social' reasons, last thing at night, from the cellar which was at ground level. Occasionally an invisible force would restrain and restrict mum or her son from descending the stairs to open the door for the dog. In the end they had to ask the others to perform the task. Naturally the father and daughter thought it was an excuse to duck out of this task, that is until further incidents occurred to convince them as well that all was not well here. Rushes of air were felt in bedrooms but the confirmation of a presence was achieved one day when they had all sat down to tea. To their dismay the lid of the teapot suddenly rose up without warning and floated in the air for quite a time before coming to ground. Fortunately they were regular chapel-goers, attending the hospital chapel in Southernhay where Father Brown was in charge. He came to the house, performed an exorcism and all was well once more. It later transpired that the house had been lived in by a medium, this being thought to be the cause of the trouble.

Evans Above, A Ghost by Gadd!

Smythen Street is a back street that runs parallel, on the south side, to Fore Street. Some years ago a large corner property at the top end of the street was occupied by the firm 'Evans and Gadd'. The late Joyce  Maunder, who once worked here, was shocked one day when, on a staircase, she passed by an employee who had died on the premises some time before. He was also spotted by a director of the firm later the same day. At the time of going to print, and as the photo shows, the premises were derelict, taking on a very ghostly appearance. Does the building's resident ghost still appear when there are no longer people around?

Kids' Stuff

There used to be a thoroughfare, in nineteenth century Exeter, called Southernhay Lane, which led to a cemetery. In those days there were many alehouses in the vicinity and as drinks were cheap and potent many of the people whose route took them home past it were often much the worse for wear. Many though, who were in a drunken state, were sober enough to take another route home for fear of seeing the bearded glaring ghost that was often found there in the dark of night.

For years some people went the long way round until an astonishing discovery was made. The ghost, with the long white beard and a frightening glare, was nothing more than a goat that liked to stand looking over the railings of the cemetery shaking its beard. This natural activity was enough to scare some of the roughest, toughest men in Exeter, we 'kid' you not!

Murder Most Foul – 'A Woman's Throat Cut From Ear to Ear'

Sidney Alford, who once lived at Thornpark Rise, was born at the beginning of the twentieth century. When he was about ten years old, just before the First World War, his parents rented a three-storey terraced residence at Lee's Terrace, a row of houses that once existed off Coombe Street, in that part of Exeter often referred to as 'the West Quarter'. This was always regarded as a tough part of the city, an area of tenements where many buildings became slums and were demolished. Many of the people who lived here were rehoused on new council estates farther out from the city centre. However, things have a way of going full circle – this area now has some excellent housing.

Sidney shared an attic room with his brother, they being just two members of a family of seven. Soon after they had moved in the boys knew that something wasn't quite right about the house. There were occasions when, mounting the stairs between the second and third storey, one of them would be picked up off the ground by an invisible force and thrown back down the stairs! This happened to several of the children but, surprisingly, none of them were ever hurt or injured in any way by this violent action.

The children's parents were sympathetic to their children's plight and allowed the two brothers to have their pet terrier in their bedroom to sleep.

One moonlit night just after the boys had gone to sleep, first one then the other suddenly woke up aware of a commotion in their bedroom. A chamber pot was being thrown around and a cupboard door was banging for all it was worth. The boys' natural reaction was mirrored by the dog for all three dived under the covers until all the banging stopped and everything returned to normal.

This story was revealed to the now defunct *Exeter Weekly News*, a paper which featured these details in 1984. Sidney Alford added that the hauntings were the probable reason why the family soon moved to new accommodation in another part of the city. He also added his belief, maybe based on something that he had heard then, that a murder had been committed in the house. He was right!

A murder did take place at the house off Coombe Street on 28 August 1895 when a family of three lived in a single room there. A woman, Emma Harris, was murdered by her husband after he had lost his temper. Their arguments were almost a daily occurrence, their neighbours being so used to the noisy confrontations that little notice was taken of them. Even the police were aware of the friction between the sparring couple as both parties had been to them to report the other for the grief they were being caused during their domestic strife. However, on that fateful late-August night things got completely out of hand when Emma struck Frank Charles Harris a severe blow with a poker. It wasn't enough to knock him unconscious and he responded by wrenching the poker from her hand and dealt her a blow that stunned her. He then, cold-bloodedly, took out a penknife, sharpened it on a leather strap and, as the headline in the local newspaper stated, cut her throat 'from ear to ear'. The body of Emma Harris, an appalling spectacle, was discovered by a young neighbour, Emily Hawkes, whose mother had sent her to the Harris's room to collect washing, which she did for the family. The police and other authorities were duly summoned to the grisly scene. Immediately Harris was arrested and charged with his wife's murder. His case took place in November and was over inside a day. The motive for the killing was deemed to be jealousy, his wife having formed a close relationship with a relative of her husband. Although the death sentence was passed this was later commuted to life. No doubt the poor victim, referred to as a sickly, feeble woman of small stature, was troubled by the outcome. Perhaps this is why she haunted poor Sidney Alford all those years ago. The property, and many surrounding ones have long since been demolished as part of a slum clearance programme and we haven't heard of any more trouble at the spot.

We felt it was quite a coincidence that, having read Anne James' excellent book *Murders & Mysteries In Devon*, we have here yet another murder story concerning a character called Harris as in Ms James' book there are six Victorian murders, four of which feature a Harris as a central figure of the story. To find yet another, and from the same era, is most surprising. One difference though is that this was a straightforward case whilst her tales have a twist or two in them.

Exeter, even in Victorian times, was not regarded as a dangerous place in which to live. This murder was the first to have occurred in the city for sixteen years, the previous one, in 1879, being by a mother of her child. She had tried to get rid of the child's remains at Trew's Weir but was being watched so carried them upstream to Bonhay Road where she tried again. She had aroused suspicion and was arrested on the spot.

A Ghost with a Hart!

Along with several colleagues, a young lady who worked at the White Hart Hotel in South Street spotted, on two occasions, the ghost of a young girl, possibly in her early twenties, wearing a long black cape that almost reached down to the floor. This solid-looking spook gave the game away when she walked up through the courtyard into South Street by ascending a set of stairs, at the front of the building, that was no longer there!

Part of this historic inn is referred to as Bottlescreu Bill's. Here a ghostly face has been sighted at the corner of the bar. It is that of a child, about four to five years old, and resembles a painting. When it has appeared, those seeing it have needed to be quick to take it in because it soon vanishes. Many people have apparently seen ghosts at this pub, close to the position of Exeter's former South Gate.

A Hair Raising Tale!

The late Theo Brown was a wonderful lady who was an expert on Devon's folklore and ghosts. She was enthusiastic about recording stories of ghosts and furnished us with one that she had recently discovered.

She had made an appointment to visit a hairdressers' shop in Exeter that was built beside Exeter's Roman wall. Instead of the normal, "Where are you going for your holiday?" conversation the topic turned to ghosts and their very existence. The stylist had no doubts for this hairdressers' 'emporium' was haunted!

A new girl, unaware of the various presences, was the first to arrive one morning at the end of her first full week. As she had a key, she let herself in to get on with the job of making the place ready for the day's styling and trimming. As she walked up the stairs she was shocked to find an invisible force pressing strongly against her, it being on the way down a flight that was too narrow for two people to pass by comfortably. The others at the salon tried to assure her that the ghosts were not bad spirits but she resigned from the job the following week.

Others who have worked there have actually seen a ghost. Appropriately this is a Roman soldier wearing a short red cloak, but although footsteps have also been heard, nothing much has happened on these premises in the last few years.

Dark Deeds in Magdalen Street

Magdalen Street has undergone vast changes since the last war. Originally its western end finished with a T-junction at the top of Holloway Street and the bottom of South Street. Here there was a pub called The Valiant Soldier with underground toilets outside and a row of shops opposite. These were tall buildings with several storeys above, mostly used as living accommodation for the shopkeepers. Names like Honeywill, Warne and Retter are just some that spring to mind.

In one of these dwellings an attractive young girl was asked to baby-sit and, as the parents were not due home until the small hours, the girl was to sleep in the house overnight. As Saturday night passed into Sunday morning she dozed off on a downstairs settee. Her slumbering was rudely awakened by the breath of a man, dressed all in black, who was leaning over her. Immediately she jumped up, in a blind panic, only to discover that all the doors and windows were tightly shut and there was nobody in the room with her! She went upstairs to check her charges were all right and when day dawned vowed never to set foot in the house again. Even now, many years later, when the buildings have all gone to be replaced by a hotel, her hackles still rise when she passes the location of her bad experience.

Good Shepherd, 'Bad Girls'

Near the Acorn roundabout is a wall, which partly conceals 'The Home of the Good Shepherd'. This was originally a charitable home for young girls who had become pregnant out of wedlock in an age when such an occurrence was viewed in anything but a charitable manner.

Having spoken to several folk who have worked there (in more recent times) we are informed that it is a place which has its spooks. They said there was a 'presence' which made them feel decidedly uncomfortable and it was not uncommon for the fire alarm to go off suddenly without any reason. And, of course, there were tales relating back to the home's former function. Rumour has it that that, many years ago, a meeting of Governors was witnessed by some of the girls who sadly slipped from their precarious vantage point to fall to their deaths in a well, which once stood beside the main building. It is felt that their spirits haunt the place and are the cause of occasional mayhem.

Creepy Colleton Crescent

Georgian Exeter was a lively, bustling trading place with much trade evident in and around the town. Founded on the wealth generated by the merchants were fine rows and crescents of Georgian town houses rising in grand style at Southernhay, Barnfield and several other locations just outside the city walls. Colleton Crescent was another fine example with tall elegant houses beautifully located on the high river cliff above Exeter Quay. This Georgian crescent was named after the Colleton family who owned all the land in this area, Miss Louisa Colleton laying the foundation stone on 3 September 1802. The crescent took twelve years to complete and has, ever since, provided quite a landmark for anyone approaching the city from the direction of the Exeter Canal.

Rumours abounded in the past of a network of secret underground passages leading from the cellars of these dwellings down through the natural cliff to the Quay. There was a strong suggestion that smugglers, with casks of rum (their term for this being 'stingo'), chose their moments to avoid the alert eye of the Coastguard or Customs men when engaged in the trade of illicitly importing goods that would have incurred dues.

In the gently curved terrace is a haunted house and we have positive proof from various sources that the property was 'busy' with ghostly activity during the 1940s and late 1950s in particular.

Mrs B., now of Clyst St Mary, moved in for a temporary period about 1957 and her first experiences involved a ghost whose footsteps would be clearly heard but nothing or nobody was to be seen. The footsteps were unmistakably ghostly for they followed her around; they would follow her upstairs and downstairs and if she stopped they would stop a short distance behind and occasionally clothes could be heard rustling. Mrs B.'s pet Pekinese would always respond to the steps and its ruff would rise up. However, this was a non-spooky spirit as it gave off pleasant vibrations and there was certainly no drop in temperature to accompany it.

There were times, however, in that period of occupation, when the footsteps were so loud when approaching that Mrs B. would mistake them for somebody who was real and would begin to say, "Hello ..." only to find nobody there.

Mrs B. was not put off by these incidents and accordingly refurbished the top flat in the house for her own occupation. Outside on the landing there was a loose floorboard, which creaked so much when anyone walked over it that it drove her to distraction, so she nailed it down very securely and promptly covered it with carpeting. When a friend arrived for tea, knowing the rest of the building was 'open house' to all and sundry, she decided to ensure their privacy by locking the door. A little while later they both clearly heard the sound of footsteps approaching them across the landing, the firmly nailed down floorboard creaking as loudly as ever it had done, and the Yale lock on the door turned. The door opened and banged close again and, of course, on inspection there was nothing there. The guest, naturally, turned ashen white but Mrs B. assured her that there was nothing to worry about.

Her fiancé, as he was then, knew all about the spirits of the house for he had spent time there in the house alone and was frequently disturbed. One night there was so much noise going on that it disturbed his sleep and he really thought that there were intruders. He searched the house thoroughly and found absolutely nothing, not a sign of life anywhere and so he went back to bed. Within seconds all the noise and banging around began again and he was so annoyed that he opened the door and bellowed down, "Shut up!"– and they did!

In the winter of 1958 Mrs B. arrived back at Colleton Crescent and parked her car in the garage, which was at the rear of the premises. It was a still, moonlit night and although there were some bare apple trees in the garden they cast little shadow so the visibility was clear. When Mrs B. saw the outline of a caped gentleman silhouetted against the bright night sky, complete with tricorn on his head, she didn't think too much of it, as it was not unusual for people to be dressed in period costume in this vicinity. She entered the gate and passed close to him but as she turned to lock it, he vanished in an instant! She firmly believes that this must have been a ghost from the past when these great houses no doubt witnessed many dramatic episodes.

Confirming her own theories on the house, Mrs B. later discovered, by chance, that the house had been used by various families during the war and it seems that a high proportion of them had to be moved out because they complained about the haunted happenings. A psychic researcher was called in but, despite various examinations, found nothing.

Ghostly Prospects

Ady Taylor, assistant manager of The Prospect Inn, stated that there were at this Exeter Quay pub, "… all sorts of banging, crashing and tapping noises, which have no explanation, loud enough to make you think that someone is trying to break in." He recounted a strange happening that took place in the early 1990s when Frank and Helen ran the pub. They stacked a tall pile of empty beer barrels at the back of the inn. However, one that had been concealed by the stack had miraculously levitated itself over the mountainous stack in front of it and was found on the ground spinning. Nobody could have done this as a prank!

However the most established ghost at this pub is of a young girl, from Victorian times, who only appears in a room at the top of the building. This is on Christmas Day when she appears clutching a soft toy, smiling and then fading into oblivion until the next festive season ... or so it's said. An electrician working there recently saw the ghost of the girl and her rag doll at an unseasonable time of year. He dropped his tools and fled.

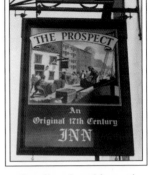

'High Spirits'

Tim Hughes runs 'Kettles' cafe, housed in the antiques centre at Exeter Quay. This he has done since the building, the old fish market, which was virtually derelict, was converted to its present use in the late 1980s. In his early years of trading there his routine

often saw him arrive early on winter mornings when there was nobody around except for a presence, which he could feel and certainly hear but not see. Until about 1993 he kept hearing a young lad whistling sea shanties, the noise sounding a little distant but emanating from the rafters. This would tie in with another trader who had seen this ghost, a curly-haired youth, sitting in those same rafters. Tim has a mental image of the youth, involved in Exeter's maritime port trade, being the victim of a fatal accident when a cargo toppled onto him. Nevertheless the spirit is not a sad one and no bad vibrations have been felt by those who have either heard or seen him. Other traders have noted, in many different parts of the building, heavy or fixed items being moved or lifted and dogs 'Barking at things that aren't there!'

Cobblestones and Creepy Customs

Next to the Custom House on Exeter Quay is Singer's Coffee Shop, run by Maria Thompson. Picture the scene one wet, winter's evening when poor Maria had driven all the way home, after a hard day's work, with the intention of later baking cakes for the next day, only to discover that the eggs she was going to use had been left behind at Singer's. There was nothing for it other than to drive once more through the wet city

streets back to an almost deserted Exeter Quay. She got out of her car and headed the few yards for the locked door of her cafe but was aware of the distinct sounds of horses' hooves on cobblestones and turned to her right to see the most unusual sight of two horses pulling a flat-backed wagon. On board was a driver who was oblivious to Maria's presence for he continued through the night towards

the Custom House, driving his horses and carriage right into the building! It scared Maria witless and as soon as she got inside her cafe she locked the door. Several minutes later she plucked up enough courage to make the short dash to her car leaving the scene as fast as she could. She is adamant that she would never go back there after dark again and who could blame her!

Historic Ghosts

The sound of ghostly, clattering hooves has also been heard travelling across the nearby medieval Exe Bridge towards the city's ancient West Gate. However, in this case the rider or the horses have never been seen.

Another unusual ghostly vision seen along Exeter's waterfront is that of a Viking vessel, which supposedly sails up the Exe, complete with a Viking King, an obvious Scandinavian stereotype of those days of yore, raising his fist defiantly at any spectators. It has been mooted that he is coming to Exeter, possibly to place a curse on the city but most probably to avenge the death of his daughter who was, apparently, murdered here.

Next to Mine Own Ship – Another One

Where Holloway Street ends and Topsham Road begins there has been a lot of redevelopment in recent years, particularly on the west side of the road. The Ship Garage, Exe Dry Cleaners and the Artillery Inn, amongst others, have all been demolished to be replaced by the new apartments of Colleton Court and Mews. However, this transition wasn't without its problems for when the workers were building the new homes several heard mysterious voices, some were even touched by invisible

hands and there was such an air of concern that the local curate was summoned to say prayers on the site. It's believed that the location was a plague pit, being well outside the city wall, the spirits perhaps resenting the disruption to their resting place. Apparently the curate of St Leonard's swift intervention did the trick and there were no further problems.

Ghostly Gun Shots

The St Leonards area of Exeter has many fine Victorian houses, ones that were built for wealthy families who had servants to do their bidding. One of these houses had many problems in the first years of the twentieth century. One unusual manifestation was the sound of a gunshot punctuating the silence of an upstairs building, this with nobody there and no damage to walls, floors or ceilings. People walking along the road outside sometimes could see that in an attic window a pair of hands were visible, put together as if prayers were being said. When this was drawn to the attention of the householders they knew it was just another ghost.

One of the children in the family who lived there was so accustomed to the sights and sounds of ghosts that she took little notice of them. Each night there was the same recurring scene. As she lay in bed she could hear the sound of the cellar door opening. Footsteps would then mount the stairs but at the same step there would be the unmistakable sound of a stumble before the footsteps continued on up into the haunted attic. The girl who lived there would often stand on that step, which always gave her a sharp, stabbing pain between her shoulder blades. Was this where a stabbing took place, the person making it to the attic before dying from stab wounds?

Although the family were accustomed to these goings on, visitors to the house sometimes could not cope with these hauntings, several refusing to come back for another visit.

Times have moved on, these big houses no longer being practicable propositions; like so many others in St Leonards, this one has been converted into flats so if you suspect that the footsteps you hear every night are not human ones … now you know the truth!

The Nude Ghost of Chestnut Avenue

Streaking is often regarded as a modern occurrence, a cunning stunt to draw attention to one's more obvious charms and accoutrements. But now we know that ghosts can do it as well. Chestnut Avenue is a long road that runs parallel with a part of Wonford Playing Fields, a quiet sort of haven and a most unlikely venue for a spiritual sortie. However, one of the avenue's residents, Mrs R., saw the ghost of a nude woman, carrying a pink nightdress over her arm, walk across the room. She was a lady who was aged somewhere between 50 and 55 years. Mrs R. noticed that the ghost had big brown eyes and brown hair but was in something of a sorry state. Her face was ashen white, and she had large tears rolling down her cheek and blood dripping from the side of her face. Standing at the foot of the bed the agonised apparition looked at Mrs R. and promptly walked right through a solid wall, never to be seen again.

This particular house has known ghosts before and since, when a man has been seen walking out from a cupboard in the bedroom, only to disappear as quickly as he appeared.

'Ghost Brings Terror into City Home'

A lady in the Wonford district of Exeter suffered such frightening hauntings that, in desperation, she turned to us to try and help her in her desire to be moved by the Council.

She was in bed one night and her husband was downstairs. Having just put out a lamp she was immediately aware of a figure nearby. The grim spectre was an old man sporting a tall top hat, like that of an old-fashioned undertaker. The ghost gripped her feet and proceeded to try and pull her out of bed until her screaming and yelling brought her husband racing upstairs, and the ghost disappeared. But worse was to come one afternoon, in broad daylight. She was lying on the settee when a pair of hands came over the top and started pulling at her neck, a terrifying ordeal that she survived, but the attack has understandably left deeply rooted psychological scars. The unearthly entity has also tried to smother her and did more than enough to warrant a change of environment for this troubled lady.

Her house was close to the Crematorium in Topsham Road and this may be significant. She heard tell that the area is haunted by the ghost of an undertaker who stalks the area trying to get some retribution for the way in which he was treated after his own death. It appears that he had expressed a wish to be buried but was in fact cremated.

Well, how do you help a person in such a predicament? Firstly the local vicar is worth contacting with a view to perhaps performing an exorcism and of course there is publicity in the local press, which might bring forward other stories to corroborate hers. The press stories which resulted threw up some interesting parallels, not least from a woman in the same road who had moved into what she believed to be a happy house only to encounter a period when several horrible things happened to her baby; it was moved from its cot onto the floor, and it was buried in its bedclothing in a way that could only have been caused by outside intervention.

Fortunately this sort of predatory ghost is rare but we should all take heart that good usually triumphs over evil.

Poor Rosa of Rutherford Street in the Wonford district of Exeter is a registered blind person and spends a lot of time at home listening to local radio, her real contact with the 'outside world'. She has lived for more than ten years in this street but has been aware, all the while, that there has been a presence in her house. In 1995 she told us that the presence was beginning to trouble her and that her sister, when paying a visit, believes she saw the same 'undertaker' but, as she watched him, he faded away. This address is within walking distance, even for a ghost, of the other haunted house.

An Horrific Haunting in Hanover Road

Hanover Road runs along the south side of the Higher Cemetery and is the location of one of the most persistent hauntings to be described in this book.

Although the family had lived in the house for quite a few years, strange things only began to happen a few years ago, a short time after a Shillelagh, regarded as an Irish lucky charm, had been introduced into the house. Initially they were fairly innocuous happenings: feelings of a presence upstairs; footsteps heard going upstairs; closed doors apparently opening themselves; and the family cat was rendered a nervous wreck. Then more sinister things started to happen.

The household consisted of a mother, father and two grown up daughters. One night, at about 3.00 a.m., the mother noticed a light on the landing and assumed that it was one of her daughters visiting the bathroom. It first of all puzzled her that she heard no obvious noises, and then she noticed how the light didn't so much turn off as simply drift away. Curious at such a strange occurrence she looked in on her daughters and found them both in a deep, sound sleep.

Soon afterwards, at the same time of early morning, one of the girls was woken suddenly. She was perspiring heavily yet was chilled to the bone by the frightening experience she then endured. A bright light shone directly into her face whilst a force pinned her down to her bed, the immense pressure leaving a burning sensation, and she was unable to speak. Henry, their dog, barked wildly and then wisely ducked for sanctuary under the bed. Fortunately everything subsided and the light and the force departed. The rest of the household laughed off the event and the poor girl was accused of having had a bit too much to drink, which didn't amuse her!

However the terrifying experience was repeated again a short time later and this time there were distinct red marks on her ankles where she had been pinned down, proving her story. Understandably she refused to sleep there again, and she swapped places with her Dad. He decided to take the cat in with him but was taken aback at the strenuous efforts made by the feline to decline the invitation. She went straight into

The Ghosts of Exeter

a corner under the bed and was found standing on her back legs with her paws spread open, her eyes as large as saucers and her fur standing up on end, like the prickles of a hedgehog. Inevitably Dad endured exactly the same experience as his daughter but bravely persevered for three weeks with only one more visitation. On that occasion the 'visitor' also tried to speak but was quite incoherent.

When this was mentioned to the next door neighbour she too recalled an occasion of hearing what she thought was her husband coming home and opening the wardrobe doors, at 3.00 a.m., two hours before usual. Needless to say, when she called him, he wasn't there!

One night a boyfriend came to stay for the night and was put in the room, it now being vacant as the other daughter had moved out of the house completely, refusing to stay in it. Once again, at 3.00 a.m., he was awoken by an immense pressure on his tummy whilst little lights danced around in front of his eyes. He couldn't move or talk for a few minutes, which seemed like an eternity to him. Immediately he was released he went downstairs, splashed water on his face to help bring himself to his senses, and promptly left the house. For a few days afterwards he suffered from a burning feeling in his stomach, which had been caused by the acute pressure applied to it.

The Shillelagh has now been removed as someone told the family that it was very unlucky to have a symbol of an opposite religion in the house, and the trouble has reduced considerably. The remaining daughter can sleep reasonably peacefully, provided the light is left on, but if the father occupies the room he is still woken suddenly by the sound of his alarm clock being thrown across the room, regardless of where he positions it.

An Uplifting Experience

Susie came to Exeter in order to take a course at the University of Plymouth! This apparent contradiction can be easily explained because the former art college in Topsham Road comes under the umbrella of the newly-created University of Plymouth in order to run degree courses. Like many students this young lady gravitated to 'student land', that semi-twilight zone of Exeter forming a circle of Victorian and Edwardian houses in a ring around the city centre, sometimes referred to as 'Bedsit Land' on account of the number of students living here. You can always tell the houses for they are invariably terraced, and have a number of door bells, stacked above each other like lift buttons. This part of the city has revealed more than its fair share of spooks.

Susie was a new recruit to this lifestyle, and had only been in Exeter a week or so, a well-spoken sensible girl who had chanced across one of our many ghost books and, out of despair, gave us a ring to tell of her first encounter with the supernatural in a flat in Monks Road. She has described her experience, for want of a better term, as a 'visitation'. As she lay in bed in a state of semi-sleepiness, a tall young lady, of about 21 years of age, appeared in her room. She was surrounded in a halo of light, wore a long white dress and hovered some way above the floor. She beckoned to Susie and as she did so she felt herself rising off the bed. By now Susie was sufficiently awake to resist the obvious influence that had been placed on her and her will was sufficient for her to drift back onto the bed.

The White Lady of Athelstan Road

Athelstan Road runs parallel to Western Way and derives its name from a Mediaeval king who did much to build up the city's defences against possible raids by the Danes. In one of its many tall houses an old lady in a white gown has been known to come through one wall and disappear through another. This has been witnessed on several occasions by a young man who previously did not believe in ghosts – he does now!

Stand and Deliver at the Vicarage

In Old Tiverton Road there is a retirement home, which was formerly the Rectory of St James. The now departed wife of a former vicar, Mrs Green, was quite sure that she saw the ghost of a highwayman, resplendent in all his customary garb for the road. Until the early nineteenth century this road was the main road to Tiverton – it was then replaced by a route cut along the river at Cowley. Therefore the haunting highwayman may well have worked this important routeway into Exeter. Various theories have been put forward as to why he has chosen this precise location. One is that the former Rectory was located on the site of the gibbet where the highwayman was hanged and the other notion is that the oak door of the building has been fashioned from the wood of the tree on which the highwayman was executed.

Whipton's Farming Ghost

Many years ago, long before the electronic age, Whipton was a quiet agricultural backwater quite removed from Exeter. This was a distant spot well beyond the city limits and the long hill known as Mount Pleasant. There were farm buildings where the Picture Palace, the takeaway and other shops now stand, although the Half Moon existed for travelling wayfarers. In this proximity a farmer, or farm worker, who fell on hard times, became so distraught at his plight that he committed suicide, and his unmistakable, dated agricultural but ghostly shape has been spotted, until quite recently, in the area around these shops.

Fairfield Avenue's Fair Maiden – A Ghost Ahead of Her Time!

There is a quiet, refined cul-de-sac called Fairfield Avenue on the outer edge of Whipton, close to the old Exeter by-pass. Originally there was an old and rambling house called 'Fairfield' at this point, which gave its name to the road. The growth of Exeter's suburbs made land on the outer fringe of the city more valuable and the house, complete with its grey lady ghost, was demolished. However, in the same road there are houses which have experienced paranormal activities. A few decades ago the ghost of a girl was seen sitting on the stairs of one of the houses. She got up, went upstairs and promptly disappeared. The girl was identified as the daughter of the previous family who had lived in the house and, although they had gone to the Cheshire area to live, the girl was known to still be alive and well. Strange indeed!

Visitors to another house in Fairfield Avenue often complained of a sudden cold feeling which made them uneasy and made them suspect that the house had some dark secrets. Out of curiosity they set up a session with a Ouija board and were overwhelmed with the response. A woman called 'Amy' answered and went into great detail about the battle in Pinhoe between the Danes and the Saxons which took place in the year 1001. After being given a graphic and lucid account of the proceedings, the family decided that it was unwise to proceed further. Since then the house has not been troubled.

It's Only Wilf – a Guardian Angel!

Causey Gardens in Pinhoe is as neat and attractive a place to live as any other residential thoroughfare in the city. Originally it was a short close but the ever outward growth of Exeter meant that land in Pinhoe became valuable building land so Playmoor Nurseries and their acres of greenhouses gave way, in the 1960s, to what is now a select housing development. After Daisy's husband died she sold her bungalow in Hampshire and moved down to Exeter to be near her son and his family, having found a very nice little modern house in Causey Gardens. She expected to have to make adjustments and everyone rallied around to make sure she settled down – including the ghost of her husband! She is adamant that on at least one occasion he appeared, as large as life, at the top of her stairs. She said she felt nothing strange about seeing him there, she believes he was simply satisfying himself that all was well with her and that she was happy. Indeed, she made friends and was quite content during her time in the house and Wilf had no need to come and check on her again.

Daisy spent a few happy years in the house but as she became an advanced senior citizen, she chose to go and live in the sanctuary of a retirement home in North Devon in 1979.

However, that isn't quite the end of the story for this house changed hands several times in the 1980s and '90s, a succession of young families living there, presumably without any 'problems' until Barry bought the property. His five-year-old child had been talking to an old man who appeared to be gentle, pleasant and friendly. Barry worked out for himself 'the Daisy Connection' (or is it Daisy Chain?) and realised that his family must be living in the same house as 'Wilf'. Some detective work on his behalf led to the location of a picture which featured Wilf in it. Without any hesitation, prompting or discussion, as to why the five-year-old was being shown a picture, the child pointed at the photo and correctly picked Wilf out as the 'man he talks to'. However, Barry stressed it was mere curiosity that put him on the trail and, even though the adults can't see or hear him, they know their resident ghost was a kindly man so have no intention of trying to remove him. Whether or not as the child gets older 'Wilf' will disappear remains to be seen, but we do know that at the time of writing, Daisy is pushing on towards her 100th year, and maybe when the time is right, Wilf will move on by himself.

Brush Strokes – The University Ghost

Some people will go to enormous lengths to strive for perfection in their work and will 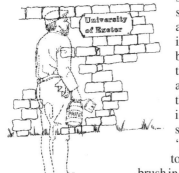 settle for nothing less than a job well done. Constantly striving for such standards can become an obsession and obsessions invariably make such an indelible impression that when the poor mortal dies he comes back again and again to relive the obsession. This is thought to be the case at the University of Exeter where a painter and decorator haunts some of the buildings on the campus. He appears complete in white overalls and is always seen gazing admiringly at his handiwork. It seems that the precise details of this story have been 'glossed' over but it is believed this man was devoted to his work and he was never happier than with a paint brush in his hand and miles of corridors and acres of university rooms in which to display his talents. This ghost appears as a solid apparition until he suddenly dissolves – a touch of the old 'white spirit' perhaps?

The Cat Who Had Ten Lives!

Newport Lodge Caravan Park lies on the border between Topsham and Exeter and is tucked snugly beneath the M5 at the point where it flies over the Exe Estuary. It was once the site of a large country house. The Todd family moved there in the late 1970s and for a time enjoyed the company of a delightful old pussycat who belonged to a neighbour. Alas, the cat used up its full quota of nine lives and duly departed to that great moggyland in the sky. After a brief 'paws', however, different members of the Todd family kept seeing the unmistakable form of the former feline. In case you think it was merely another cat they were seeing, on occasions just half of the departed cat appeared!

I Beg Your Pardon

On another occasion, Mr Todd, at the end of a long and tiring day, wearily set off into the darkness to walk across Newport Caravan Park. However, in his tired state, he was not as alert as he normally was and he was brought up short when he bumped into a passer-by. Startled by the impact, he immediately started to apologise – until he realised he was speaking to thin air!

The Devil in Topsham

Topsham has been visited by the Devil on at least two occasions and obviously is a place where he feels very much in his element. Whether or not this is because of the vastly disproportionate number of pubs and the associated revelry and high jinks that go with drinking, is not known. However, many years ago at a pub called The Railway Inn a group of typical locals engrossed in their game of Sunday night cards had a frightening experience. One man dropped a playing card, which fluttered to the ground, but as he bent down to retrieve it, he had his hand immediately pinned to the floor by the Devil! A frantic struggle followed between the man's friends and the Prince of Darkness  until he was eventually released amidst the turmoil. The card players and other onlookers fled in fear from The Railway Inn and, in keeping with the Devil's behaviour in such situations, he started to vandalise the building by demolishing an end wall of the inn completely! The building was repaired but was never re-licensed for spirits after that!

Topsham's 11.30 p.m. Ghost

In *Dark and Dastardly Dartmoor* you can read about a strange ghostly phenomenon that was encountered at Moretonhampstead – a haunting which took place, regularly, not at the witching hour of midnight but at 9.15 p.m. Topsham has its own variation with a ghost which used to appear on every occasion at 11.30 p.m. The ghostly grey figure would rise out of the ground in the road near a church. It would drift slowly down the road until it reached the graveyard where it promptly disappeared only to reappear down the road to start the spectral journey again on its next outing. It was particularly active until June 1968 but has been scarcely seen since then.

Read All About It!

The west side of the River Exe also has its ghosts!

Perriam's is a well-known newsagent's shop in Cowick Street, a business which has prospered since about 1914 under various owners. Originally it was a coaching inn and until early this century had a stable block at the back. It only requires a glance to see that it is an old building with a long history, an ideal location for ghosts!

The first recorded haunting was experienced by Mrs Sedgemoor who, with her in-laws, ran the business earlier this century. The resident pet was a little Scottie dog called Jock, a canine critter who had formed a distinct bond with Mrs Sedgemoor. One evening when she was sitting down with Jock nestled against her she heard what she believed was her mother-in-law returning home from an evening walk. It sounded as if the front door was 'tried' and Mrs Sedgemoor called out. Jock sensed something and got as close to Mrs

S. as possible. Mrs S. was so convinced that someone had appeared that she called out but there was nobody there. Soon afterwards the little dog became petrified and snuggled up even more closely to Mrs S. Within seconds the presence, which had caused this fear, passed over the lady's shoulder. She felt it but did not see it.

The building continued to throw up its malevolent forces. Mrs S. and her mother-in-law, Mrs Perriam, decided that they needed more storage space and an understairs cupboard, which had not been used for years, seemed to be the ideal choice. When the two ladies gained entry they both had such an over-whelmingly terrible feeling that they couldn't stay in there, despite the fact that the potentially valuable space was 'as clean as a whistle'. It was quickly re-sealed with a six inch nail.

Mrs Perriam died in about 1950 but is believed to have returned to the house long after her death. The evidence for this lies in the perfume which she loved to wear at all times. She would buy a scent called 'Jonquil' (French for daffodil) from a chemist called Wynne Tighe and Son in St Thomas. The unmistak-able waft of Jonquil would suddenly fill the air but yet again nobody was seen.

Mrs Sedgemoor has psychic powers with an ability to tell fortunes – she has used her skills to raise money for St Loye's in the past – and has also had many premonitions. She witnessed a most unusual ghost at Perriams when she saw the head and shoulders of a darkly coloured, 12-14 year old Indian boy. It was seen by a bottle and jug window and hovered for several minutes at a height about level with the picture rail. Although she drew her husband's attention to it, he couldn't see it.

Her last spectral sighting at the newsagent's occurred in the 1950s when the face of a scruffy, heavily weathered old man appeared in front of a picture which was hanging on the wall. After several minutes the gnarled but animated old face just faded away never to be seen again.

These particular incidents were well covered by the media. When the press tried to set up a picture to reconstruct the scene, Mrs S. was quick to point out that the fabricated picture they created was far more gruesome than the phantom itself!

Now You See Me

This following story was recounted by a very sane gentleman from Ide. He was returning from a spot of late night fishing on the canal one night when, driving along the stretch of road from the Devon Motel towards Marsh Barton along Bad Homburg Way, he had a most unusual experience.

It was in the early hours of the morning and ahead of him on the road he could see a vintage car motoring very slowly. As he gained on the vehicle a gauntleted hand appeared out of the window on the driver's side and waved him to overtake.

The passing motorist had time to study what appeared to be a very old but interesting vehicle as he passed by. However, a split second later when he pulled in after overtaking and glanced in his mirror, the vehicle had vanished – and on closer inspection he saw absolutely nothing on this clear, open stretch of road!

A Ghost at Library HQ – Long Overdue!

Barley House is a distinct man-made landmark high on the hills of Redhills. This late Georgian building became the county Library in 1939 and now acts as the Library Headquarters, a building which is 'just the ticket' for such a purpose.

The site of the building provides a perfect view of the lower Exe Estuary and many miles of countryside can be seen from its lofty vantage point, despite the fact that Exeter has grown up to and well beyond it. The first house established on the site was built several hundred years ago. It was garrisoned by Fairfax whilst he besieged Exeter in 1646 at the close of the English Civil War. The present building was built about 1800 and was originally known as Barley Mount and, as a house, has had some distinguished residents.

Formerly Barley House had fine extensive gardens, which extended way down the hill, now Isleworth Road, to its junction with Buddle Lane. Where the line of shops is at the bottom were the drive gates. Children in the 1920s and '30s could earn a ha'penny by opening these gates for a carriage or automobile arriving from Exeter or one of the large country houses in the vicinity. These would have included Cleve House, Crossmead, Reed Hall and so on. But it wasn't only carriages and automobiles  that the children should have kept an eye out for – because there was also the ghost of a lady in grey.

Early in 1940, not long after the library had moved in, the caretaker, who lived in a flat on the first floor, heard the sound of sobbing coming from outside. He went to investigate and saw a woman dressed in grey crying and in a state of great distress. As he approached, in order to offer assistance, she vanished before his very eyes. The experience obviously had quite a profound effect on him because soon after, when a similar incident occurred again, he decided it was time to move on and neither the lady, nor the caretaker, has been seen since – perhaps the ghost was equally shocked by the experience!

However, strange footsteps are often heard and heavy doors have been known to slam shut in what are regarded as draught free conditions. Mr Hunt, who was the former County Reference Librarian, kindly supplied these details and is quite adamant that the old house 'had a life of its own after dark'.

The Cowick Barton Ghost Will Look After You!

Two low-lying areas of Exeter are Exwick and Cowick, both on the same side of the river and both hamlets sited, long ago, on the edge of the River Exe's flood plain. Cowick is old and has an interesting history dating back to at least a mediaeval settlement or perhaps even older. In the twelfth century the land upon which Cowick Barton is built belonged to Cowick Priory, a religious house located beside the Exe in what is now Okehampton Street.

The Cowick Barton public house was probably the priory farm, being sited on much better ground. The agricultural pursuits were curtailed as Exeter's residential growth spread outwards to encompass the Cowick Barton. In 1963 it was bought by a brewery when it was a derelict farmhouse. Soon after it was licensed for spirits, other kinds of spirits also started to appear.

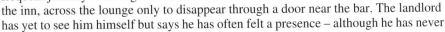

The pub is well known for its ghostly monk, a most benign, gentle spirit who has made a 'habit' of appearing to people who are ill. It is believed that when the monk was in this mortal coil he tended the sick with loving devotion and has continued to do this even beyond the grave. He has a quiet, reassuring countenance and has been seen on numerous occasions in his dark coloured habit. His most frequent journey is through the front main door of the inn, across the lounge only to disappear through a door near the bar. The landlord has yet to see him himself but says he has often felt a presence – although he has never felt scared.

The pub has another ghost, that of a Royalist soldier who has appeared to many guests in their bedrooms. Like many ghosts, his favourite act is to lean over people when they are asleep as if trying to see if they are well. It obviously hasn't occurred to this old Cavalier that if the sleeping guests were to awaken he might well scare the wits out of them! However, those who have been roused have survived to recount that he is a mild spirit and they were not afraid.

Taxi!

Late night-time taxi driving, even in a relatively quiet city such as Exeter, can be quite a challenging job. Conveying passengers in various states of rationality – sometimes too friendly, sometimes too aggressive – to their homeward bound destination can make a driver confident that he or she has seen it all before.

It was 2.00 a.m. and Frank Cook was enjoying a well-earned break whilst waiting for his next fare, parked outside Bowhill House, which is at the junction of Bowhay Lane near Dunsford Road. Originally it was the seat of the Holland family who were related to the Dukes of Exeter.

Suddenly, Frank's quiet period of reflection was interrupted by a rush of wind and a distinct, definitely uncomfortable, feeling of someone being in the cab with him. To his amazement the car ignition then switched itself on and all the ignition and warning lights on the dashboard flashed into life. Scared witless, he decided not to hang around and drove off into the night away from the invisible 'fare' who was far more of a menace than the usual night-time customers!

Now you have been introduced to just some of the ghosts that roam our fair city, some more pleasant than others. We hope you have enjoyed these armchair encounters. Just remember you may well be the one in ten to have your own close encounter, perhaps tonight! Don't panic, it will give you something to talk about for the rest of your life or even beyond…